String Time Christmas

16 pieces for flexible ensemble

Kathy and David Blackwell

MUSIC DEPARTMENT

OXFORD
UNIVERSITY PRESS

OXFORD
UNIVERSITY PRESS

Great Clarendon Street, Oxford OX2 6DP,
United Kingdom

Oxford University Press is a department of the University of Oxford.
It furthers the University's objective of excellence in research, scholarship,
and education by publishing worldwide. Oxford is a registered trade mark of
Oxford University Press in the UK and in certain other countries

First published 2019

Impression: 1

ISBN 978-0-19-352805-5

Music and text origination by Julia Bovee
Printed in Great Britain on acid-free paper by
Halstan & Co. Ltd, Amersham, Bucks.

Credits

Recording credits: *Violins*: Ros Stephen and Rebekah Allan; *Viola*: Louise Hawker;
Cello: Laura Anstee; *Double bass*: Rory Dempsey; *Piano*: David Blackwell; *Drums and
percussion*: Ben Twyford.
Recorded at Oxford Brookes Recording Studios. Producer and audio edit: Ken Blair.
Recording engineer: Will Anderson. A bmp production for Oxford University Press.
Cover illustration by Martin Remphry.

Contents

* These carols may be played separately.

Welcome to String Time Christmas!

Who is the book for? Young string players in groups of all sizes and at different skill levels, from approximately Grades 1–2/3. The parts are all in 1st position and there are some optional 4th position notes for the cello.

What's in the book? A range of seasonal pieces, including traditional Christmas carols, carols from around the world, and Classical pieces. A medley of three traditional carols makes a longer piece, or each carol may be played separately.

How does the scoring work? Most pieces have two main parts—parts 1 and 2—which can be played by **violin**, **viola**, and **cello**. Occasionally there are small variations between the different instruments to accommodate finger patterns and ranges. To simplify the presentation of the score, both these parts are written in the treble clef, but of course the cello will play an octave lower. There's also an optional **double bass** part, and a **piano** part which is optional in some of the pieces (Nos. 3, 4, 12, and 16). Some pieces also have additional optional parts, e.g. a violin descant or separate cello part. **Percussion** can be added to any of the pieces for extra sparkle, e.g. some sleighbells in the Mozart 'Sleighride' (no. 15).

What does 'flexible ensemble' mean? The pieces can be performed in a variety of ways to suit different groups, from duets in any combination to massed strings. For example, all instruments could play the tune in unison with the piano, or cellos could take the tune with upper strings on the accompanying part 2, or all instruments could split into two parts, with or without the additional optional parts. Some sections could be taken by solo players. Most of the pieces could also serve as accompaniments to singers too. Repeat each piece as many times as you like!

How do I play 'Christmus a-come'? Choose the melody plus any of the other parts and play as many times as you like. The piece could build up, adding more parts each time, or players could keep to one part and play from the start. Or players could *swap* parts on each repeat, playing like a kind of round (e.g. imagining parts 1, 2, and 3 as a 24-bar round and played by three groups entering every 8 bars).

Are there any recordings? Yes, audio files (performance and backing tracks) are available to download from www.oup.com/stchristmas, using the code in the front of the book. The violin, viola, and cello books all contain access codes for the audio files, but these are not available for the double bass book, so teachers should feel free to share their audio downloads with the double bass pupils in their ensemble.

What books are available? This book contains the score and piano part, and there are separate books for violin, viola, cello, and double bass.

Happy Christmas!

Kathy and David Blackwell

1. We wish you a merry Christmas

English trad.
arr. KB & DB

vn descant (opt.)

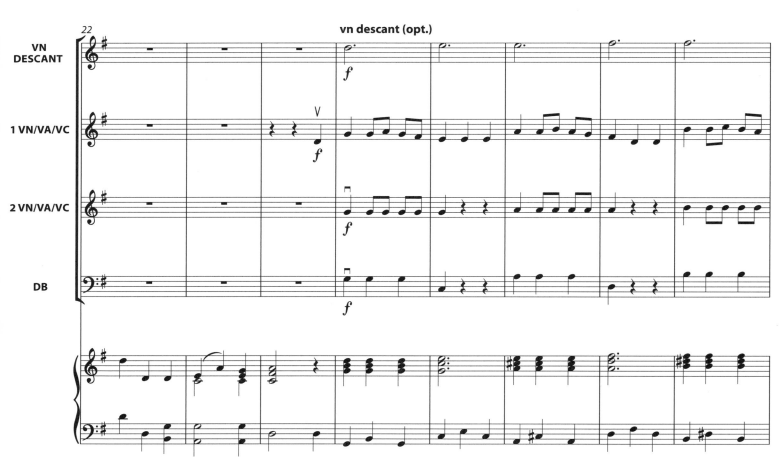

2. Away in a manger

W. J. Kirkpatrick (1838–1921)
arr. KB & DB

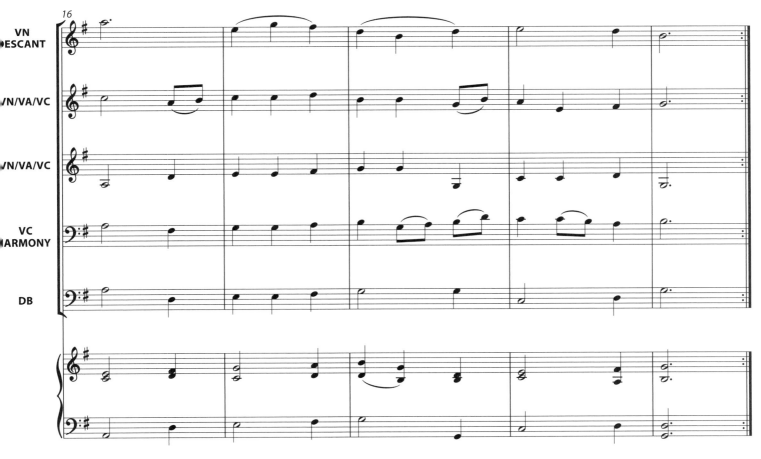

3. Deck the hall

Welsh trad.
arr. KB & DB

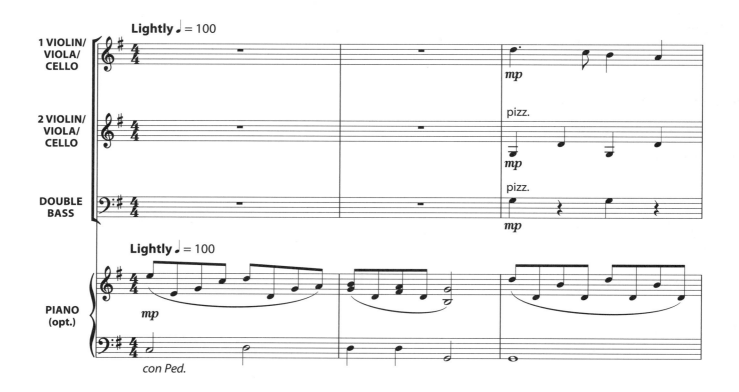

4. Hark! the herald-angels sing

F. Mendelssohn (1809–47)
arr. KB & DB

5. Silent night

F. Gruber (1787–1863)
arr. KB & DB

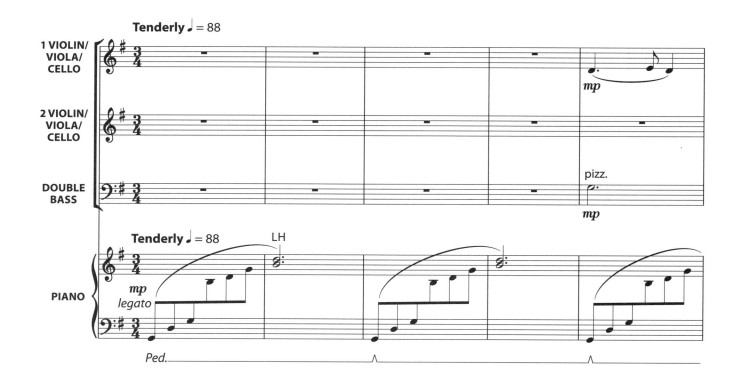

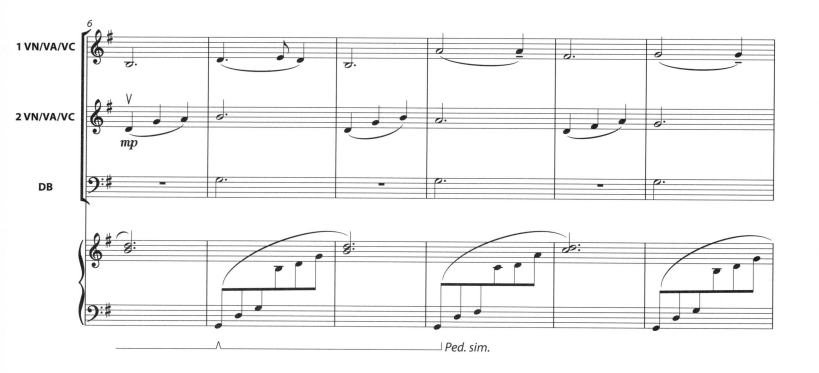

6. Christmas Medley

arr. KB & DB

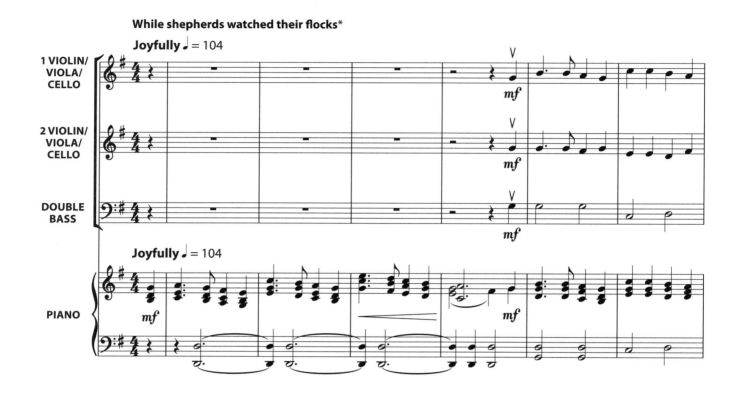

* English trad., from Este's Psalter (1592)

O little town of Bethlehem*

* English trad.

* Melody from *Piae Cantiones* (1582)

7. Ding dong! merrily on high

16th-century French melody
arr. KB & DB

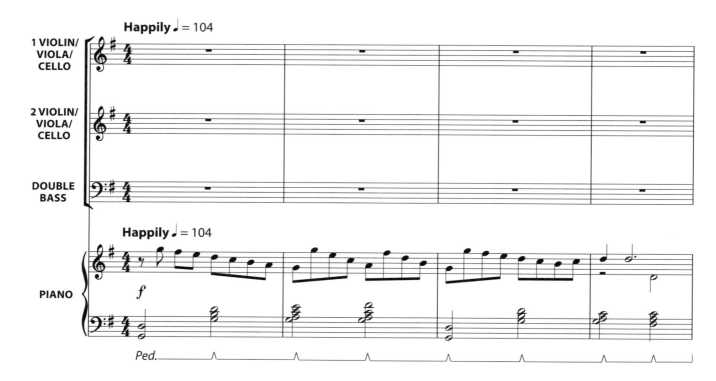

8. El Noi de la Mare
The Child of the Mother

Catalan trad.
arr. KB & DB

9. Go tell it on the mountain

Spiritual
arr. KB & DB

String Time Christmas

16 pieces for flexible ensemble

piano accompaniment book

Kathy and David Blackwell

Contents

* These carols may be played separately.

MUSIC DEPARTMENT

OXFORD
UNIVERSITY PRESS

1. We wish you a merry Christmas

English trad.
arr. KB & DB

2. Away in a manger

W. J. Kirkpatrick (1838–1921)
arr. KB & DB

3. Deck the hall

Welsh trad.
arr. KB & DB

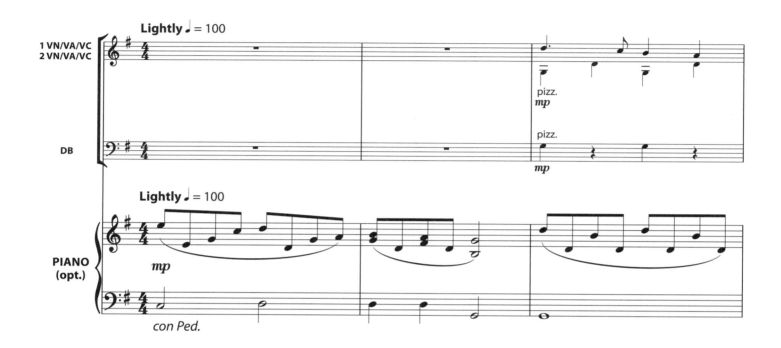

4. Hark! the herald-angels sing

F. Mendelssohn (1809–47)
arr. KB & DB

5. Silent night

F. Gruber (1787–1863)
arr. KB & DB

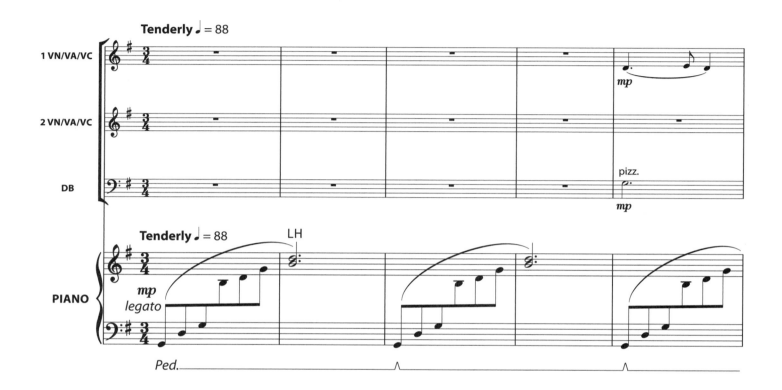

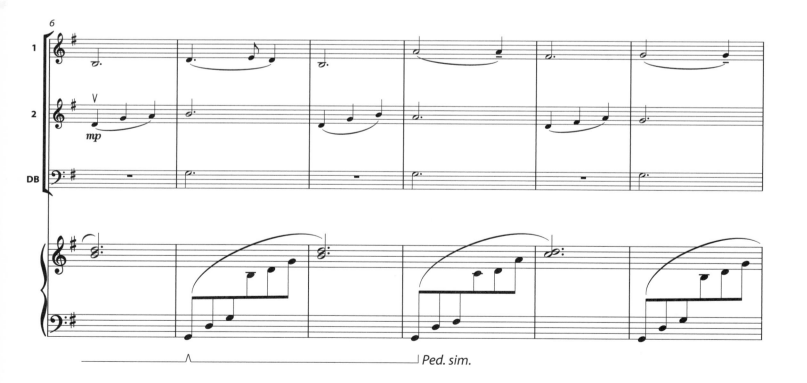

6. Christmas Medley

arr. KB & DB

While shepherds watched their flocks*

* English trad., from Este's Psalter (1592)

O little town of Bethlehem*

* English trad.

Good King Wenceslas*

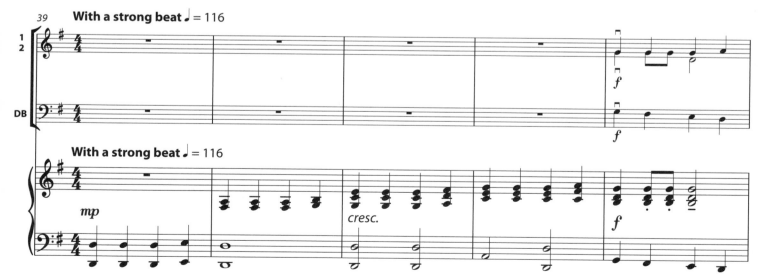

* Melody from *Piae Cantiones* (1582)

7. Ding dong! merrily on high

16th-century French melody
arr. KB & DB

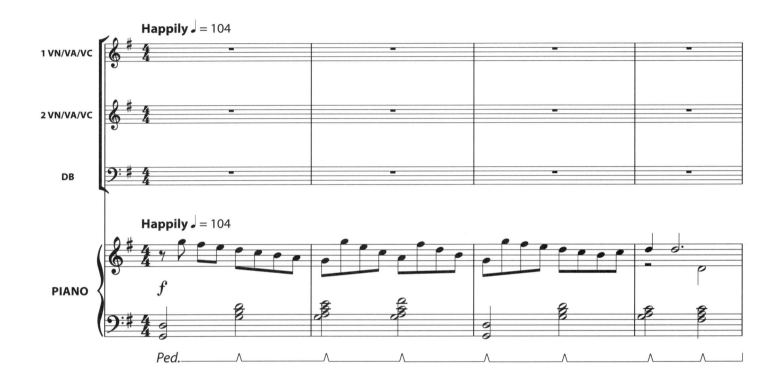

8. El Noi de la Mare
The Child of the Mother

Catalan trad.
arr. KB & DB

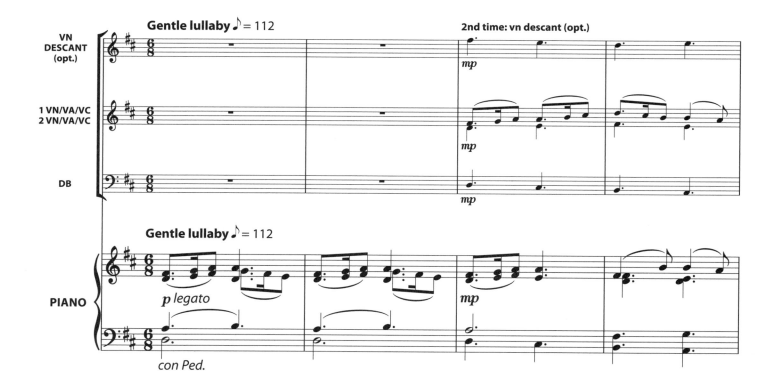

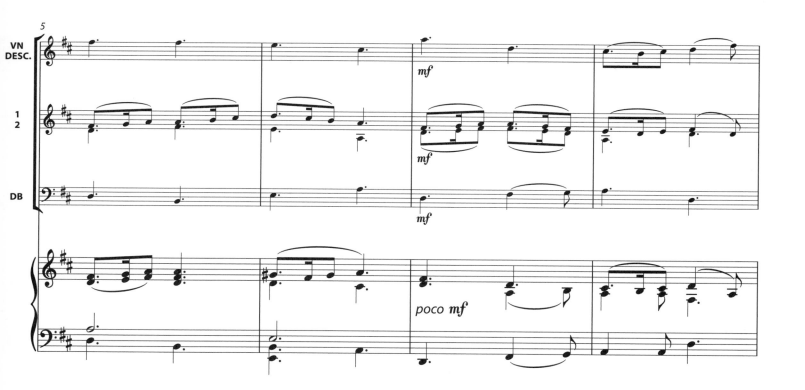

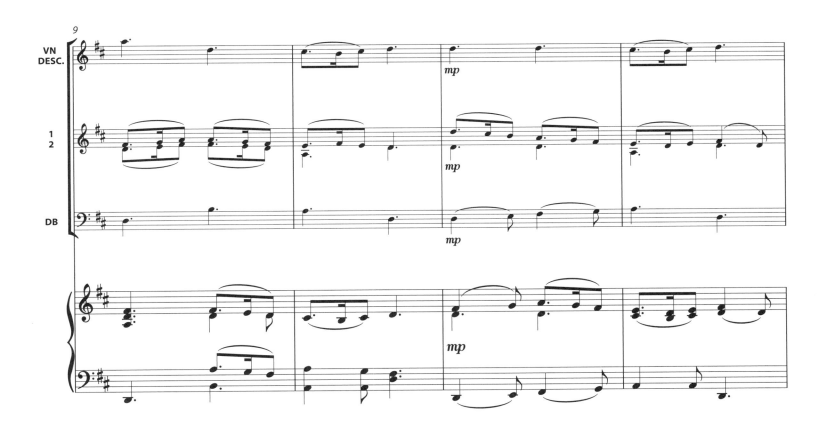

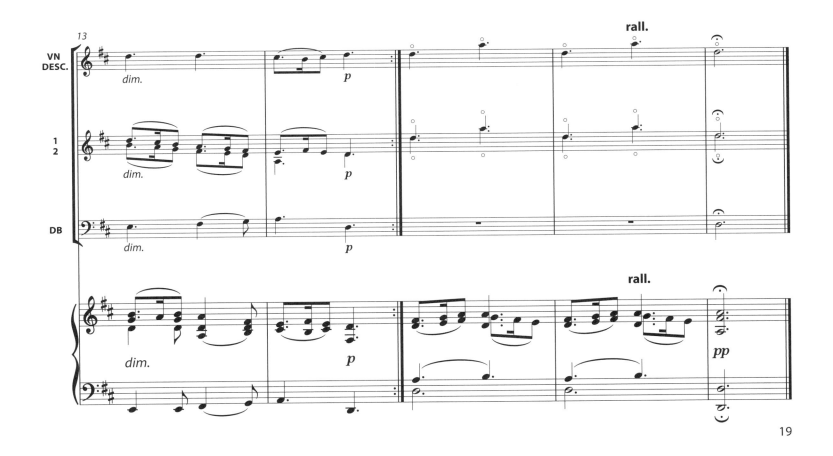

9. Go tell it on the mountain

Spiritual
arr. KB & DB

Tell it on the moun - tain!

11. The Virgin Mary had a baby boy

Caribbean trad.
arr. KB & DB

Piece no. 10 is on page 26.

10. Cantemos a María
Let's sing to Mary

Dominican Republic trad.
arr. KB & DB

12. Huron Carol

Canadian trad.
arr. KB & DB

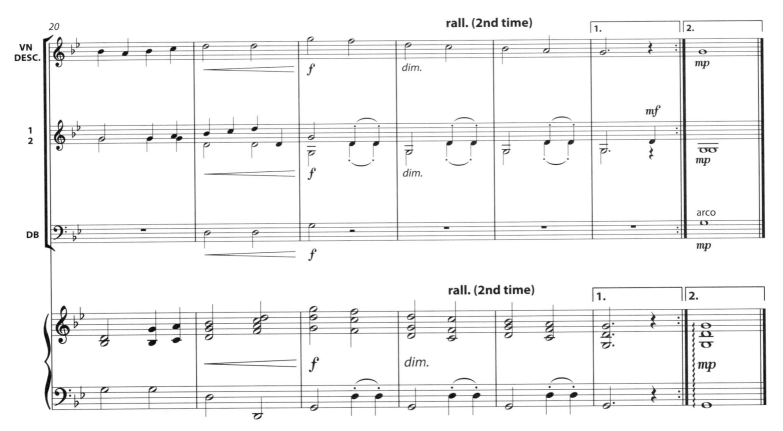

13. Joy to the world

G. F. Handel (1685–1759)
arr. KB & DB

14. Trepak
from *The Nutcracker* ballet

P. I. Tchaikovsky (1840–93)

arr. KB & DB

15. Sleighride
K. 605

W. A. Mozart (1756–91)

arr. KB & DB

16. Chrismus a-come

Jamaican trad.
arr. KB & DB

26

10. Cantemos a María
Let's sing to Mary

Dominican Republic trad.
arr. KB & DB

12. Huron Carol

Canadian trad.
arr. KB & DB

Piece no. 11 is on page 32.

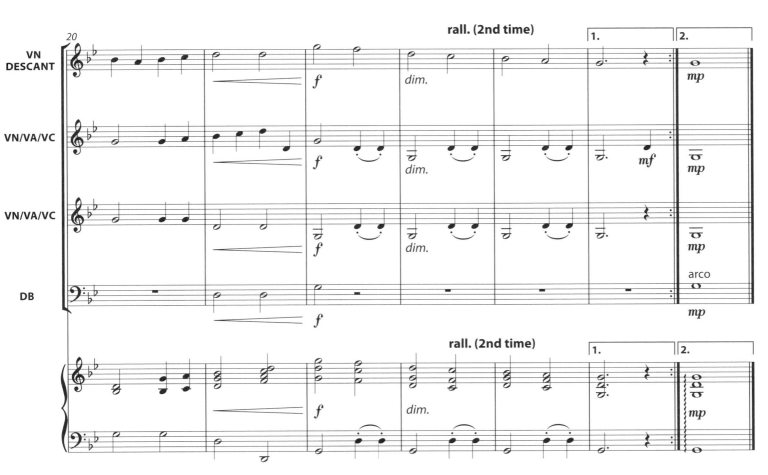

11. The Virgin Mary had a baby boy

Caribbean trad.
arr. KB & DB

13. Joy to the world

G. F. Handel (1685–1759)
arr. KB & DB

14. Trepak
from *The Nutcracker* ballet

P. I. Tchaikovsky (1840–93)
arr. KB & DB

15. Sleighride
K. 605

W. A. Mozart (1756–91)
arr. KB & DB

The D.C. should be played without the repeats.

16. Chrismus a-come

Jamaican trad.
arr. KB & DB

Chris-mus a-come, I wan - na go home, *etc.*

Chris-mus a-come, I wan - na go home, *etc.*

repeat ad lib.

opt. introduction: piano bars 5–8

repeat ad lib.

For performance suggestions, see p. 4.